Surviving Disaster:
Real Life Tales of Survival and Resilience

Surviving
PEARL HARBOR

Kira Freed

rosen publishing's
rosen
central®

New York

Published in 2016 by The Rosen Publishing Group, Inc.
29 East 21st Street, New York, NY 10010

Copyright © 2016 by The Rosen Publishing Group, Inc.

First Edition

Developed and produced for Rosen by BlueApple*Works* Inc.

Art Director: T.J. Choleva

Managing Editor for BlueApple*Works*: Melissa McClellan
Designer: Joshua Avramson
Photo Research: Jane Reid
Editor: Marcia Abramson

Creative Commons: Christopher P. Becker (p.34); Public Domain: U.S. Navy photo (cover); U.S. Navy photo by Greg Vojtko (title page, back cover); U.S. Navy photo/Photographer's Mate 2nd Class Arlo Abrahamson(p. 4); U.S. Navy (p. 8); United States Navy Photographer's Mate 3rd Class Kittie VandenBosch (p. 11); U.S. National Archives and Records Administration (p. 12, 22); U.S. Navy photo by Mass Communication Specialist 3rd Class Amber L. Porter (p. 14); US Naval History & Heritage Command (p. 17); p. 17; U.S. Navy photo (p. 19, 21, 27, 28); USAAF/Lee Embree, (p. 30, 33); U.S. Army (p. 39); Department of the Interior. National Park Service (p. 40); Army Signal Corps (p. 43); U.S. Navy photo by Mass Communication Specialist 2nd Class Laurie Dexter (p. 45); Joshua Avramson (p. 24); Shutterstock.com: LittleStocker (p.6)

Library of Congress Cataloging-in-Publication Data

Freed, Kira.

Surviving Pearl Harbor/Kira Freed.—First edition.

pages cm.—(Surviving disaster)

Includes bibliographical references and index.

Audience: Grades 5-8.

ISBN 978-1-4994-3649-5 (library bound)—ISBN 978-1-4994-3651-8 (pbk.)—
ISBN 978-1-4994-3652-5 (6-pack)

1. Pearl Harbor (Hawaii), Attack on, 1941--Juvenile literature. 2. World War, 1939-1945--Causes--Juvenile literature. I. Title.

D767.92.F73 2016

940.54'26693—dc23

2015000655

Manufactured in the United States of America

Contents

Pearl Harbor was named the permanent home of the U.S. Pacific Fleet in February 1941 and continues to serve as the headquarters of the U.S. Pacific Fleet to this day.

Chapter 1
Pearl Harbor History

Pearl Harbor is a beautiful warm-water lagoon on the island of Oahu in Hawaii, about 25 miles (40 km) west of the capital city of Honolulu. Ancient Hawaiians found the lagoon full of food: birds, fish, and pearl-making oysters. Many uses were found for the oyster shells, but it is not clear whether the Hawaiians put any particular value on the pearls inside. The Hawaiians called the lagoon Wai Nomi ("pearl water") and the surrounding land Pu'uloa ("long hill"). According to legend, Pearl Harbor was the home of the shark goddess, Ka'ahupahau, and her brother, Kahi'uka. When Europeans began arriving in 1778, a thriving trade in pearls developed, and the lagoon got its English name. Pearl Harbor was overfished and the oysters almost died out, but today they are making a comeback.

As more trading and whaling ships began stopping in Hawaii, American missionaries and their families settled in the islands as well. U.S. warships also visited the **strategic** islands. Starting in 1820, the U.S. government appointed a special agent to look after all the Americans and American businesses in Honolulu. By 1868, American naval officers were playing a key role in Hawaii.

Honolulu is the capital city of the U.S. state of Hawaii. The name *Honolulu* means "sheltered harbor" or "calm port."

They settled business disputes and negotiated trade agreements. The Hawaiian royal family was invited to travel around the islands as well as to the mainland on U.S. warships.

The original harbor was shallow, and coral reefs made its entrance narrow. In 1869, Congress appropriated $50,000 to pay for improving the harbor so larger ships could dock there, and in 1874, the king of Hawaii granted the United States the right to build a coaling and repair station for ships at Pearl Harbor. After the Spanish-American War of

1898, the United States decided that it needed a stronger presence in the Pacific. The decision was made to establish a full naval base in Pearl Harbor. The opening to the harbor was widened. Many buildings and docks were erected, including a shipyard that opened in 1908. Expansion of the base continued, and Pearl Harbor was named the permanent home of the Pacific Fleet in February 1941.

As the great naval base was taking shape, Hawaii was annexed to the United States in 1898 and remained a U.S. territory until gaining statehood on August 21, 1959.

Working Together

The U.S. Army has also had a presence on Oahu since the early 1900s. After naval facilities were established, the Army was responsible for protecting the base with aircraft as well as coastal defense artillery. The U.S. Army Air Corps—changed to the U.S. Army Air Forces in 1941—was also present on Oahu and was part of the U.S. Army. (The U.S. Air Force became a separate branch of the U.S. Armed Forces in 1947.) The Air Corps operated land-based bombers and pursuit aircraft.

The Navy operated aircraft as well. Aircraft carriers had bombers and fighter planes. Battleships had scouting and observation planes. Patrol aircraft were based on Oahu. The Marines, a component of the U.S. Navy, provided security on ships and made up ships' landing forces. Marines also served as sentries at Pearl Harbor.

U.S. Navy sailors rescued survivors near the USS West Virginia during the Japanese attack on Pearl Harbor on December 7, 1941.

Chapter 2
December 7, 1941:
"A Date Which Will Live in Infamy"

On the morning of December 7, 1941, the Empire of Japan attacked the U.S. Pacific Fleet, although the two countries were not at war. The surprise attack on Pearl Harbor was intended to cripple or destroy the U.S. fleet so it could not interfere with Japan's plans for conquest in Southeast Asia and the Pacific.

The first attack planes flew over Pearl Harbor at 7:48 AM Hawaiian time, when many people were still asleep. The raid was conducted by 353 Japanese warplanes launched from six aircraft carriers. When the attack was over, 2,300 Americans were dead. Pearl Harbor remained the deadliest attack on U.S. soil until the terrorist bombings on September 11, 2001. For many Americans, the words "Pearl Harbor" became synonymous with "sneak attack."

The deadly attack stunned Americans. Many of them had not wanted to get involved in World War II, but for most Americans that changed in a single morning. The next day, President Franklin D. Roosevelt gave his famous speech declaring that December 7, 1941, was "a date which will live in infamy" and announced that the United States had declared war on Japan.

Ninety Minutes That Made History

The Empire of Japan had joined the side of Germany and Italy, called the Axis, in World War II. Japan was looking to expand its power and influence, and it saw the United States as a major obstacle in the Pacific. The attack on Pearl Harbor was designed not only to destroy the U.S. Pacific Fleet but also to **demoralize** Americans. Japan thought that the death and destruction at Pearl Harbor would make Americans even less likely to favor involvement in the war. Instead, the attack backfired. It brought the American people together and solidified their resolve to fight back. Pearl Harbor bounced back, too. Despite the damage to U.S. ships and aircraft, the base itself was not heavily damaged, and it played a key role in supporting naval operations against Japan during World War II.

Japan had also chosen that morning to strike because the United States was about to start building more warships under a 1940 law called the Vinson-Walsh Act. Japan reasoned that if America was demoralized, those plans likely would be abandoned.

The actual attack came in two waves. Battleships and airfields were the key targets, followed by cruisers and de-stroyers. Because it was early morning, most U.S. aircraft were parked, and their pilots were not nearby. There was no time to get the planes in the air. Japanese fighter planes were able to destroy an estimated 164 U.S. aircraft, which prevented the Americans from mounting an effective airborne defense, and a massive number of **torpedoes** and bombs were launched against the U.S. battleships.

When the attack was over, ninety minutes after it began, 1,999 sailors, 233 soldiers and airmen, 109 marines, and 49 civilians had been killed. Another 1,178 people were wounded. Twelve ships were sunk or run aground, including five battleships.

Of those five, the USS *Arizona* took the hardest hit. The *Arizona* exploded and sank, killing 1,177 of the 1,512 crew on board. Some of the damaged ships were **salvaged**, but not the *Arizona*. The wreck of the *Arizona* remains underwater at Pearl Harbor as a tribute to all those who died there. It was declared a national shrine, and many people visit the memorial site every year. Pearl Harbor continues to serve as the headquarters of the U.S. Pacific Fleet.

Nearly two million people come each year to visit the USS Arizona Memorial, which opened in 1962.

The crew tried hard to save the badly damaged USS *California*, but they had to abandon ship when a mass of burning oil floated nearby.

Chapter 3
Inferno on the Battleships

In the early hours of December 7, seven American battle-ships were **moored** along Battleship Row, on the eastern side of Ford Island in Pearl Harbor. The ships represented most of the Pacific Fleet's warships and the biggest obstacle to Japan's goal of dominating Southeast Asia and the Pacific. Just before 8:00 am, Japanese Imperial Navy Commander Mitsuo Fuchida gave the order for torpedo bombers to drop their torpedoes on Battleship Row. Soon after, a second wave of Japanese aircraft dropped bombs on the battleships.

The USS *Arizona*, which sustained the worst damage, was hit by at least three bombs and exploded, causing the deaths of 1,177 crewmembers. The USS *Oklahoma* capsized after being hit by at least five torpedoes and was also a total loss, with 429 dead. The USS *West Virginia* sunk after being hit by two bombs and at least seven torpedoes, losing 106 men. The USS *California*, hit by one bomb and two torpedoes, also sunk, with 102 dead. The USS *Nevada* was hit by five bombs and one torpedo and was beached, with fifty-seven crewmembers dead. The USS *Maryland* and *Tennessee* together lost nine men.

USS *Arizona*

About half the Americans who lost their lives during the attack were on the USS *Arizona*, the first battleship to be hit. At about 7:55 AM, the ship's air raid siren sounded. Soon after 8:00 AM, ten Japanese aircraft flew over, and multiple bombs hit the ship, including at least two that damaged the middle and rear portions. However, the greatest damage was caused by a 1,757-pound (797 kg) armor-piercing bomb that struck the front of the *Arizona*.

A marble wall lists the names of all those who died aboard the USS Arizona. Visitors often bring flowers to the wall to honor the fallen.

The ship's forward ammunition supply chamber ignited, which then ignited other ammunition supply chambers. The monumental explosion seconds later created an enormous plume of black smoke and sparked fires that burned for two days.

The *Arizona* sank in less than nine minutes, taking with it 1,177 of the 1,512 officers and enlisted men. Among those who died were Rear Admiral Isaac Kidd, commander of three of the U.S. Pacific Fleet's battleships, and Franklin Van Valkenburgh, the *Arizona's* captain. The ship was a total loss, and because of the fires, only parts of it could be salvaged. The rest of the *Arizona* remains at the bottom of Pearl Harbor.

Survivor Account

Marine Corporal E.C. Nightingale was aboard the USS *Arizona* at around 8:00 AM when he heard the ship's siren sound. On the way to his battle station, a huge explosion caused the *Arizona* to shake violently and set fire to a large part of the ship. As Nightingale made his way off the ship, the impact of another bomb catapulted him into the water. He started swimming toward shore but lost strength halfway there. Major Alan Shapley, a Marine Corps officer, grabbed him and started swimming, with Nightingale gripping his shoulders. When Shapley's strength gave out, Nightingale told him to go on alone. Nightingale later recalled, "[Shapley] grabbed me by the shirt and refused to let go. I would have drowned but for the Major."

USS *California*

Just after 8:00 AM, the USS *California*—the flagship of the U.S. Pacific Fleet since 1921—was hit by two torpedoes, which caused rapid flooding, as well as by a bomb that hit the upper deck. The explosion from the bomb ignited an ammunition supply chamber and killed roughly fifty crewmembers. Another fifty men also died in the attack. Four crewmembers—more than any other ship—were awarded Medals of Honor for their service during the attack, three of them **posthumously**.

Because of smoke, it became necessary to **evacuate** the forward engine room. As a result, it was impossible to continue pumping out water to keep the battleship from sinking. Another danger was a large amount of burning oil that was floating down Battleship Row toward the *California*, which prompted the commanding officer to order crewmembers to abandon ship. The men later returned, but the flooding was uncontrollable, and the ship eventually sank. Flooding was accelerated by some of the *California's* watertight compartments being open since the ship was due for inspection.

The *California* was raised in March 1942 and returned to service in January 1944 following a salvage operation and the installation of new equipment.

Survivor Account

Navy gunner Lieutenant Jackson C. Pharris was stunned and badly injured when the first torpedo struck the *California*. Regaining clarity, he organized men to manually deliver ammunition to antiaircraft guns after the mechanism supplying them was destroyed. The ship was without power and listing severely as water and oil rushed in and oil fumes caused crewmembers to collapse. Although Pharris was himself overcome by oil fumes and in severe pain, he ordered the ship counterflooded, kept the ammunition supply train moving, and entered flooded compartments to rescue unconscious crewmembers. He survived his injuries and was awarded the Navy Cross —later upgraded to the Medal of Honor—for his bravery during the attack.

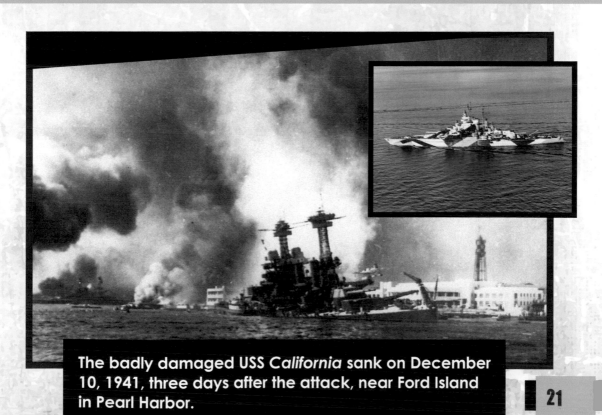

The badly damaged USS *California* sank on December 10, 1941, three days after the attack, near Ford Island in Pearl Harbor.

USS *Nevada*

The USS *Nevada* was struck by one torpedo near the end of the first wave of the attack. The battleship was fitted with an older type of anti-torpedo protection that limited damage from the warhead, but even so, a large amount of flooding occurred. Still afloat, the ship started moving toward the Navy Yard.

USS Oklahoma

USS California

USS West Virginia

USS Arizona

USS Nevada

A Japanese pilot took this aerial photo of Battleship Row just as the attack began.

During the second wave, the *Nevada* became a prime target for Japanese pilots, who hoped to sink the ship in order to block the harbor. The battleship was hit by five bombs, which caused more flooding and ignited fires in various areas of the ship. Its antiaircraft guns were still functional, so the crew attempted to protect the ship as well as move it out of the harbor so it would not be sunk. When the *Nevada* couldn't move any farther, it was beached at Hospital Point, across the channel from Ford Island. A total of fifty-seven men lost their lives in the attack. The ship was returned to service in October 1942.

Survivor Account

Warrant Officer Machinist Donald Kirby Ross was belowdecks when the **Nevada** was struck by a torpedo. He went to his station in the ship's forward dynamo room, which furnished power to keep the ship running. When smoke, steam, and heat filled the room, Ross ordered other sailors to leave and worked alone to transfer control of the power to a different part of the ship until he became blinded and unconscious. After being rescued and brought back to consciousness, he returned to his station and succeeded in transferring power. He then went to work in the after (rear) dynamo room, again to the point of unconsciousness. After being **resuscitated**, he remained at his station until ordered to abandon it. Ross's actions kept the **Nevada's** power on and prevented it from sinking or blocking the harbor. He was the first World War II recipient of a Medal of Honor.

Japanese pilots flew the Mitsubishi A6M, nicknamed the Zero. These nimble fighter planes ruled the air in the early part of World War II.

Chapter 4
Wrecking the Airports

The Japanese attack on Pearl Harbor targeted U.S. airfields in addition to battleships. While the ships were attacked to prevent interference with Japan's plans for expansion in Southeast Asia and the Pacific, the airfields were targeted to keep American planes from hindering the Japanese attack. If a large number of American planes could get in the air, they would represent a significant threat to Japanese aircraft. In addition, long-range aircraft would be able to track Japanese planes returning to their aircraft carriers, which would place those ships in jeopardy.

Japan ravaged U.S. airfields during both the first and second waves of the attack. The attack was a total surprise, and U.S. aircraft were completely unprepared, having neither fuel nor weapons. Many other aircraft had been moved from Hawaii to locations closer to the Philippines in anticipation of an attack there. Japanese bombers dropped high explosives on U.S. planes, and fighters fired cannons and machine guns. Fire also caused considerable destruction, as most aircraft were lined up wing to wing, and flames quickly spread from one plane to the next.

The airfield segment of the attack mainly focused on six locations. The first bomb of the entire airfield attack was dropped at Ford Island Naval Air Station, located in the middle of Pearl Harbor. Ford Island was a key target for the first wave of raiders. Despite losing one large hangar and thirty-three planes, including several long-range aircraft, the Ford Island airfield kept operating throughout the attack. Wheeler Army Airfield, the main fighter base, was heavily attacked, and close to two-thirds of its 140 planes were destroyed or disabled. The aircraft at Hickam Army Airfield, which was located next to the Navy Yard, saw a similar degree of damage. In addition, dozens of soldiers at Hickam lost their lives when the Japanese dropped bombs on their barracks.

Other airfield targets included Kaneohe Naval Air Station, which lost most of its aircraft—long-range PBY patrol seaplanes that would otherwise have been able to identify the location of Japanese aircraft carriers. Ewa Marine Corps Station lost more than half its planes, mainly bombers and fighters. Bellows Field was also hit and several aircraft destroyed. In total, an estimated 164 U.S. aircraft were destroyed and 159 were damaged.

However, not all U.S. aircraft were helpless in the face of the Japanese attack. Several P-40 Warhawks took off from Bellows Field but were quickly shot down. P-40s from Wheeler Field, temporarily parked ten miles away at Haleiwa Field, were more successful.

The attack decimated planes, hangars, and airmen's quarters at Wheeler Army Airfield.

The men who died at Kaneohe were buried quickly on December 8. This ceremony to honor them was likely on Memorial Day in 1942.

The Japanese, who knew the attack was a complete surprise, assumed that U.S. aircraft would not pursue them and therefore weren't alert to their presence. A total of fourteen U.S. pilots succeeded in becoming airborne and shot down at least nine Japanese planes.

Survivor Account

When Japan attacked Pearl Harbor, Second Lieutenant Kenneth Taylor's squadron's planes, usually at Wheeler Field, were temporarily parked at Haleiwa Field, an auxiliary airstrip. Taylor called ahead for the ground crew to have his and Second Lieutenant George Welch's P-40 fighter planes armed, fueled, and warmed up. Then the two soldiers got in Taylor's car and sped to their planes, taking off as soon as they arrived. They were the first two Army Air Forces pilots to get in the air and fire at Japanese aircraft. Together they shot down at least six planes. Both were awarded the Distinguished Service Cross, and Taylor also received a Purple Heart. He later said, "There were between two hundred and three hundred Japanese aircraft. There were just two of us! I wasn't in the least bit terrified, and let me tell you why: I was too young and too stupid to realize that I was in a lot of danger."

Aircraft Carriers

Japan could not have carried out such an effective attack on Pearl Harbor without the use of aircraft carriers. The idea of launching aircraft from ships had been around since 1910, but pre-World War II military strategists expected battleships to be the main weapons of war and viewed aircraft carriers simply as tools of **reconnaissance**. The lack of understanding of the powerful advantage offered by aircraft carriers sharply increased the surprise factor at Pearl Harbor. The attack was the first use of multiple aircraft carriers for a single operation. As World War II progressed, aircraft carriers and submarines proved far more important than battleships.

The B-17 bomber was nicknamed the Flying Fortress because it was heavily armed and so tough that it could keep flying after taking many hits.

Chapter 5
Hapless Witnesses

In the hours before Japan attacked Pearl Harbor, twelve U.S. Army Air Forces pilots were flying B-17 Flying Fortress bombers belonging to the 38th and 88th Reconnaissance Squadrons from California to Hickam Field. The bombers had machine guns and bombsights, but to reduce their weight so they could carry more fuel during the long flight, they did not have any ammunition. The planes were scheuled to be refueled and stocked with ammunition at Hickambefore taking off again to join their bombardment squadrons in the Philippines.

The Flying Fortresses reached Oahu only half an hour after the Japanese attack began. As the bomber pilots, crew, and passengers approached the Hawaiian Islands, they saw fighter planes flying toward them and thought that Americans were coming out to escort them to the airfield. Suddenly the fighter planes began firing at them. Without the ability to fire back, the B-17s were totally vulnerable. Two were destroyed in the air, and the other ten landed, most while being **strafed** by Japanese fighters. Several B-17s were also hit by **friendly fire** after being mistaken for Japanese aircraft.

Pacific Theater of World War II

The attack on Pearl Harbor had crippled but not destroyed the Pacific Fleet. Its aircraft carriers were away during the attack, and onshore storage, repair, and warehouse facilities were undamaged. All but three battleships were raised and repaired. Pearl Harbor quickly recovered and played an important role throughout World War II. The base repaired U.S. ships returning from battle and supplied outbound ships with fuel and provisions.

The same day that Pearl Harbor was attacked, Japan also attacked the Philippines. Over the next months, Japan quickly took control of an enormous portion of the Pacific. In April 1942, the tide began to turn when the United States conducted an air raid on Tokyo. The raid demoralized Japan, which now realized it was vulnerable to air attack. Japan resolved to destroy U.S. aircraft carriers to prevent future attacks. However, two months later, at the Battle of Midway, Japan lost four aircraft carriers in what is considered the turning point in the Pacific war.

Following Midway, the Allies went on the offensive, attacking Japan's weak points and setting up Allied bases as they island-hopped toward Japan. Starting with the Guadalcanal Campaign, Japan suffered heavy losses in one battle after another.

By late 1944, Japan was finally in reach of the U.S. Army Air Forces' new long-range B-29 bombers. Strategic bombing of Japan began in late November. More battles were still to come, but by that point Japan was all but beaten.

World War II in Europe ended in early May 1945 with Germany's unconditional surrender, but Japan vowed to continue fighting, even with little hope of winning. In late July, the Allies called for Japan to surrender and promised "prompt and utter destruction" otherwise.

In early August, with Japan still refusing to surrender, American B-29 bombers dropped atomic bombs on the cities of Hiroshima and Nagasaki, killing more than 120,000 people instantly. The bombings prompted Japan's Emperor Hirohito to surrender unconditionally on August 15. The surrender agreement was signed two weeks later on the USS *Missouri*. The deadliest war in history was finally over.

Diplomatic and military leaders of Japan officially surrendered on September, 2 1945, aboard the USS *Missouri* in Tokyo Bay.

Pearl Harbor Today

On January 29, 1964, the Pearl Harbor Naval Station was declared a National Historic Landmark. It contains many other landmarks associated with Japan's surprise attack. The USS *Arizona* Memorial, built over the sunken battleship, honors the ship and its lost crew, whose names are engraved on a marble wall. Over the years, Pearl Harbor survivors have volunteered at the memorial, helping bring history to life for visitors.

The site of Japan's surrender is also memorialized. After many years of service, the USS *Missouri*—the world's last active service battleship—returned to Pearl Harbor on the 50th anniversary of the attack and was retired there. Other visitor attractions include memorials to lost crew of two other battleships as well as the Pacific Aviation Museum Pearl Harbor and USS *Bowfin* Submarine Museum.

Pearl Harbor is still an active military base as well as the headquarters of the U.S. Pacific Fleet. It's also a place to reflect on the events that drew the United States into World War II and keenly affected an entire generation of Americans. Visitors honor and remember those who lost their lives in the attack as well as those who fought courageously in the years that followed.

USS *Arizona* survivor John Chapman (center) was an honored guest at the 2014 Pearl Harbor remembrance.

Glossary

animosity Extreme hostility.

austere Plain and harsh.

bombsights Devices on aircraft used to accurately aim bombs.

censorship The practice of reviewing material before it is made available to the public in order to remove anything considered offensive, harmful, or a security threat.

confiscated Seized property.

counterflooded Flooded compartments on one side of a ship to counterbalance the already flooded other side in order to prevent the ship from capsizing.

demoralize Cause a person or group to lose confidence, hope, or courage.

detonate To explode.

evacuate To empty; to remove the contents of.

friendly fire An attack from one's own side, often because of mistakenly identifying the target as the enemy.

internment Confinement within certain limits for political or military reasons, especially during a war.

listing Tilting to one side.

moored Held in place with ropes, cables, or anchors.

negatives Images on film used to print photographs, particularly before the advent of digital photography.

posthumously Occurring after a person's death.

reconnaissance Military activity conducted with the purpose of gathering information about an enemy.

resuscitated Brought back to a state of consciousness and activity.

salvaged Rescued after being ruined or destroyed.

strafed Fired at with machine guns from low-flying aircraft.

strategic Useful or important in gaining an advantage or achieving a goal.

torpedoes Underwater missiles designed to destroy ships by exploding and rupturing their hulls.

For More Information

Books

Tarshis, Lauren. *I Survived the Bombing of Pearl Harbor, 1941*.
New York, NY: Scholastic, 2011.

Demuth, Patricia Brennan. *What Was Pearl Harbor?*
New York, NY: Grosset & Dunlap, 2013.

Oppenheim, Joanne. *Dear Miss Breed: True Stories of the Japanese American Incarceration During World War II and a Librarian Who Made a Difference*.
New York, NY: Scholastic, 2006.

Mazer, Harry. *Boy at War: A Novel of Pearl Harbor*
New York, NY: Simon & Schuster, (2012).

Taubman, Bess. *My Pearl Harbor Scrapbook 1941*.
Phoenix, AZ: MapMania Publishing Co., 2014.

Websites

Because of the changing nature of Internet links, Rosen Publishing has developed an online list of websites related to the subject of this book. This site is updated regularly. Please use this link to access this list:

http://www.rosenlinks.com/SD/Pearl

Index